In the name of Allah, the Compassionate, the Merciful.

Ah Tesslimiyet

SUBMISSION

Sayings of the Prophet Muhammad ص

Hadith selections, Design, Photographs

by Shems Friedlander

Hadith Notations

by Al-Hajj Shaikh Muzaffereddin

Title Calligraphy, Ninety Nine Names of Allah

by Hattat Hamid al-Amidi

Arabic text written

by Dr. Tevfik Topuzoglu

(University of Istanbul)

HARPER COLOPHON BOOKS
Harper & Row, Publishers
New York, Hagerstown, San Francisco, London

Note: the letter ﺺ which follows the name of the
Prophet Muhammad ﺺ is a customary abbreviation
for the benediction salli'aLāh'alīh wa ālihī, (may the
blessings of God be upon him and his family).

Photograph page 114
by Nezih Uzel

Calligraphy, last page
by Professor Nihad M. Cetin,
University of Istanbul

Typography by
TypoGraphics Communications, Inc.

Original prints made by
Image Photo, Elizabeth Pope

Other books by
the author.
THE WHIRLING DERVISHES
WISDOM STORIES FOR THE
PLANET EARTH

First edition: HARPER COLOPHON BOOKS, 1977

LIBRARY OF CONGRESS CATALOG NUMBER:
77-4644

ISBN: 0-06-090592-1

77 78 79 80 81 10 9 8 7 6 5 4 3 2 1

This work is dedicated to
al-Hajj Muzaffereddin
Shaikh of the Tekke of Kutbul Arifin,
Gavsulvasiliyn, Hatemul Muctehidin
Sultan Muhammad Nureddin al-Cerrahi al-Halveti.

Mihrab in Mevlevi Tekke in Konya, Turkey.

Introduction

HADITH (Tradition)

Hadith is a record of what the Prophet Muhammad, may the peace and blessings of Allah be upon him, said, did or approved. It is a guide on how to live according to what was sent down in the Qur'an. The preserved information on such topics as ablution, prayer, charity, knowledge, marriage, divorce, family, business ethics, and food and drink are the basis for Islamic existence. Islam is based on the morality of man. A man must first want for his brother and then for himself.

Muhammad was given the actual words of Allah which became Qur'an. Hadith are his own words spoken from divine guidance.

Al-Bukhari was one who dedicated his life's work to compile and authenticate Hadith. It took sixteen years to select just over 7,000 hadith from the 600,000 he had learned. Other accepted authenticators of Hadith are Muslim, Abu Dawud, al-Tirmizi, Ahmad, and Ibn Majah. Others collected hadith but these six remain the most accepted. May Allah be pleased with them.

MUHAMMAD

Muhammad means the Praiseworthy. He was medium-sized with a bright face which was neither white nor brown. Revelation came to him when he was forty. It continued for ten years in Medina and ten years in Mecca. He did not have more than twenty white hairs in his head and beard. He was thick set, had broad shoulders, and his hair reached the lobe of his ear. His face was like the moon, not like a sword. His hand was more perfumed than musk. His palm was softer than silk and satin. He had the most pleasant odor. (from al-Bukhari)

'Ali adds that "he had the *seal of the prophecy* between his shoulder blades. He was the most truthful, the most generous, the gentlest and the noblest of men. Whoever saw him unexpectedly was in awe of him, and whoever spoke to him as an intimate loved him. I never saw anyone like him before or after him."

Muhammad, the son of Abd'Allah was born in Mecca fifty-three years before the Hijra. His father died during his mother Amina's pregnancy and she died while he was still a young boy. He was then cared for by his grandfather 'Abdul Muttalib until his death when his uncle Abu Talib took over the responsibility. Most people in Mecca at that time could neither read nor write which allowed for a natural development of memory. There lived poets who could recite thousands of verses without reference. Muhammad's education was informal and he worked as a shepherd in the hills surrounding Mecca. At twenty-five, under the employ of a wealthy widow named Khadija, Muhammad made a successful journey to Syria as a trader. Khadija was impressed by the exemplory character of her employee and married him. The marriage lasted twenty-six years, until her death. During that time she bore children and gave him great support during the difficult years when he was trying to spread Islam to the people of Mecca, a people formerly involved with idol worship and business profits.

In his fortieth year Muhammad was given the beginning of the revelation of the Qur'an. The turmoil in Mecca and the blessings of Medina which followed are part of history and will not be gone into here. We are interested in the application of Hadith in daily life.

When his name was called, Muhammad answered, "At your service." He himself said, "I was sent to complete the noble qualities of character." One of his names, al-Quatham, means the complete, perfect man.

DIRECTION

The Shaikh is the living example of the Message delivered by the Messenger. The dervish is like a honeybee and the Shaikh is the flower. Not all bees are honeybees. A flower may be good for one honeybee and not another. The bee must know what is sweet to him.

The Shaikh is ahl-ul ha qa'iq, he who knows the truth. Whatever he says is by virtue of his knowledge and his silence is deference to his maturity. The power of his heart is made alive by dhikr. Those in his company know that dhikrullah satisfies all hearts. He does not say one thing and do another. His way is the way of the Messenger of Allah.

Sema, salat, dhikr, the wearing of dervish clothes are all external. They are personal and only benefit the person doing it. These are all aspects of being a dervish. *To be a dervish is to help others.*

Many years ago in Medina there was an argument between a shopkeeper and his customer. In those days, all the shops were open to the street. So when the shopkeeper, in a moment of uncontrolled anger, slapped the customer it was in front of witnesses. One slap in the face and when the man hit the ground he was dead. A crowd formed. In those days, justice was immediate. If you killed someone then your life was taken.

The man said, "I only slapped him. I did not intend to kill him, but I know the law and I also must die. Before I am put to death, I have one request. There are two orphans in my care and I would like the time to arrange for them to be taken care of and to inherit my property." "This is impossible," said the judge, "you have killed a man, you can't leave this place."

Finally, after some of the gathering was heard from, the judge agreed to a postponement if the man could find someone to vouch for him. He looked out into the crowd which now numbered hundreds, and stopped at the face of a man. "He will vouch for me," the shopkeeper said, extending his finger toward the man. "Will you vouch for this man?" asked the judge. The man glanced around until he was certain the question was for him, then replied, "Yes."

The man was taken into custody and the shopkeeper rode off on his horse. "Do you know the shopkeeper?" the judge asked. "No." "Then you must have known the man who was killed." "No," answered the man. "But I don't understand. Do you realize that you have vouched for this man and if he does not return it is you who will die?" "I understand this clearly," replied the man. "Then what made you risk your life like this?" "The shopkeeper was in great difficulty. He looked out into this vast crowd and chose me. Out of these hundreds of people, he chose me to help him. It was not possible for me to refuse."

Hours passed. The gathering was filled with anxiety. The shopkeeper had not returned. Finally the dust from his horse was seen and soon after he rode into the marketplace. "Forgive me for being late," he panted, "but it took this long for me to find someone who would agree to care for the orphans."

The judge and the crowd were so moved by the honesty of these two men that they called the family of the man who died, and asked if the shopkeeper could be forgiven. The family agreed.

This is Submission. This is the kind of relationship that we do not even speak of now.

The Gnostic of Allah, Pir Nur-eddin Cerrahi of the Halveti Order of Dervishes in Istanbul, may Allah be pleased with him, wrote a "Lesson in Perfection."

> With inner care from your heart be pleased and thankful to
>   Allah.
> One with such faith, if he prays, he will see the light.
> With salat and dhikr he will become light.
> A person who loves the truth will tell the truth.
> He who acquires this knowledge, his sins melt and he is
>   cleansed.
> One who becomes the Tawid, his heart becomes larger than
>   the universe.
> When you see a poor creature, do not look at him with disdain.
> He who has pride, gets destroyed.
> Don't give your heart to the world.
> He who lets himself be caught by the world falls far from
>   Allah.

It is the job of the Shaikh to lead people to God. They will be led according to how open they are. The Shaikh can be very close to God. If you take a glass of water from the sea, what is in the glass is not the sea, yet it is the sea. This is how the Shaikh is to God.

It is the hope that this work not only be treated as a collection of great sayings but as a practical guide to daily life. The Names of Allah have been written phonetically to enable those who do not know Arabic to receive the blessing of repeating them. Each Attribute can be worked with. They are filled with opposites for He is the Constrictor and Expander; Majesty and Beauty. Know Allah by His Attributes, know that all things come from Allah and that there is no strength save Allah.

Each hadith can be taken and applied to life. It is time to change our attitudes into aptitude, to apply ourselves to the Straight Path. Adam was the first man and the first Prophet. He was chosen by God. In Arabic, the name Adam is made from the letters alif, dal, and mim, which represent man standing, bowing and prostrating. When man prostrates to God it is the only time that his heart is above his head. Our life's conditioning and education stress intellect as the means to livelihood and the solution to problems. Islam shows that the heart is the answer to all questions. I heard Halveti Shaikh Muzaffer of the Cerrahi Tekke in Istanbul say, "God no longer wants philosophy, He wants love." I heard him say that "flying and walking on water are miracles, but a mosquito can fly. What is important is to find a direction. The Qur'an, the words given through the Prophet Muhammad is a direction for man."

Hu is a name for God. We are hu-man, we are divine man and God will only accept divine love, the love of a man whose heart is above his head.

Any shortcomings in this work should be attributed to me. May I be judged by my intention and may all those who know more be inspired to come forth and extend this work.

Astaghfiru'llah!

Shems
New York City, Ramadan 1397 Hijra
September, 1977

Transliteration

ʾ	ء	ḍ	ض		short vowels	
b	ب	ṭ	ط	´	:	a
t	ت	ẓ	ظ	و	:	u
th	ث	ʿ	ع			
j	ج	gh	غ	◌	:	i
ḥ	ح	f	ف		long vowels	
kh	خ	q	ق	ا..	:	ā
d	د	k	ك			
ḏ	ذ	l	ل	..و	:	ū
r	ر	m	م	..ى	:	ī
z	ز	n	ن			
s	س	h	ه			
sh	ش	w(u)	و			
ṣ	ص	y(i)	ى			

Note: To make the reading of the Arabic proper names easier, the diacritical marks have been omitted.

AR-RAHMAAN

The Beneficient

A'ishah reported that Harith ibn Hisham asked Allah's Messenger, "How does revelation come to you?" "Sometimes it comes like the ringing of a bell, which is the hardest on me, then he departs and I remember what was said. At other times the Angel speaks to me from the likeness of a man and I remember what was said."

A'ishah said, "I saw him receive revelation on an extremely cold day, and when it departed his forehead dripped with perspiration."

[Transmitted by Bukhari]

Note: This ringing may correspond to the ringing of a telephone or a ringing sound in one's ear. When the receiver is lifted the ringing stops and the message comes through.

The physical changes which affected the Prophet during his receiving revelation should not be regarded as epilepsy as some tend to believe. He received these words in a clear state as verified by the text, "I retain in memory what is said."

عَنْ عَائِشَةَ أَنَّ الْحَارِثَ ابْنَ هِشَامٍ سَأَلَ رَسُولَ اللهِ ﷺ فَقَالَ يَا رَسُولَ اللهِ كَيْفَ يَأْتِيكَ الْوَحْيُ فَقَالَ رَسُولُ اللهِ ﷺ أَحْيَانًا يَأْتِينِي مِثْلَ صَلْصَلَةِ الْجَرَسِ وَهُوَ أَشَدُّهُ عَلَيَّ فَيَفْصِمُ عَنِّي وَقَدْ وَعَيْتُ عَنْهُ مَا قَالَ وَأَحْيَانًا يَتَمَثَّلُ لِيَ الْمَلَكُ رَجُلًا فَيُكَلِّمُنِي فَأَعِي مَا يَقُولُ.

AR-RAHEEM

The Merciful

THE MESSENGER OF ALLAH, peace and blessings of Allah be on him, has said: "In the body is a piece of flesh, which when good, the entire body is good; when corrupt, the entire body is corrupt; it is the heart."

[Reported by Nu'man ibn Bishr]
[Transmitted by Bukhari]

عَنِ النُّعْمَانِ بْنِ بِشْرٍ . . . . . .
اَلَا وَ اَنَّ فِي الجَسَدِ مُضْغَةً اِذَا
صَلَحَتْ صَلَحَ الجَسَدُ كُلُّهُ وَ اِذَا
فَسَدَتْ فَسَدَ الجَسَدُ كُلُّهُ اَلَا
وَ هِىَ القَلْبُ .

AL-MALIK

The Sovereign Lord

THE MESSENGER OF ALLAH, _{peace and blessings of Allah be on him,} has said: "Worship Allah as if you see Him; if you do not see Him, know that He sees you."

[Reported by Abu Hurairah]
[Transmitted by Bukhari]

AL-QUDDOOS

The Holy

THE MESSENGER OF ALLAH, peace and blessings of Allah be on him, has said: "Islam is built on five pillars.

Affirmation that there is no god but Allah and that Muhammad is the Messenger of Allah.

Prayer performed five times each day.

Zakat, a tax for the needy to be given a year after it is earned.

Hajj, the pilgrimage to Mecca.

Fasting, from dawn to sunset throughout the month of Ramadan every year."

[Reported by Ibn 'Umar]

[Transmitted by Bukhari]

Note: *Zakat* – hoarding money in Islam is forbidden. Money should be circulated to the benefit of others.

عَنِ ابْنِ عُمَرَ قَالَ قَالَ رَسُولُ اللهِ صلى الله عليه وسلم بُنِيَ الْإِسْلَامُ عَلَى خَمْسٍ شَهَادَةُ أَنْ لَا إِلهَ إِلَّا اللهُ وَ أَنَّ مُحَمَّدًا رَسُولُ اللهِ وَ إِقَامِ الصَّلوةِ وَ إِيتَاءُ الزَّكوةِ وَ الْحَجُّ وَصَوْمُ رَمَضَانَ.

AS-SALAAM

The Source of Peace

THE MESSENGER OF ALLAH, _{peace and blessings of Allah be on him,} has said: "None of you has faith unless he loves for his brother what he loves for himself."

[Reported by Anas]
[Transmitted by Bukhari]

AL-MOMIN

The Guardian of Faith

THE MESSENGER OF ALLAH, ^{peace and blessings of Allah be on him,} has said: ''None of your faith is complete unless I am dearer to him than his father, his son and all mankind.''

[Reported by Anas]
[Transmitted by Bukhari]

عَنْ اَنَسٍ قَالَ قَالَ رَسُولُ اللهِ صلى الله عليه وسلم لَا يُؤْمِنُ اَحَدُكُمْ حَتَّى اَكُونَ اَحَبَّ اِلَيْهِ مِنْ وَالِدِهِ وَ وَلَدِهِ وَ النَّاسِ اَجْمَعِينَ.

AL-MUHAIMIN

The Protector

THE MESSENGER OF ALLAH, ^{peace and blessings of Allah be on him,} has said: "When a person is drowsy during his prayers, let him go to sleep until he knows what he recites."

[Reported by Anas]

[Transmitted by Bukhari]

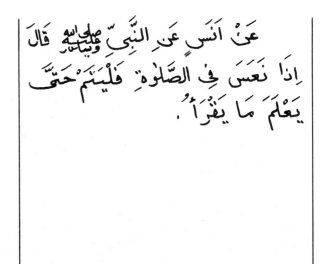

*The circle of dhikr
begins with the Name of
Allah, for His Names
are a fortress invincible
against harm. (Sidi 'Abd
al-'Aziz Hilali of
Marrakesh)*

The Shaikh must know when his dervishes are ready to be open. This is the most important part of dhikr. At this time the Shaikh says ''qalbit'' and the dhikr must automatically come from the heart. The sound changes to a heavy breath or ''sawing'' dhikr.

In dhikr one cannot copy the sound and manifestations of another. The true movement must come as if you are devoured by the dhikr. Mevlana Rumi likened sema to a vulture coming down to eat its prey.

AL-AZEEZ

The Mighty

THE MESSENGER OF ALLAH, ^{peace and blessings of Allah be on him,} has said: "Whoever offers prayers as we do, faces the Qiblah and eats the animal slaughtered by us, he is a Muslim for whom is the covenant of Allah and the covenant of the Messenger of Allah; so do not violate Allah's covenant."

[Reported by Anas]
[Transmitted by Bukhari]

عَنْ اَنَسٍ قَالَ قَالَ رَسُولُ اللهِ صلى الله عليه وسلم مَنْ صَلَّى صَلَاتَنَا وَ اسْتَقْبَلَ قِبْلَتَنَا وَ اَكَلَ ذَبِيحَتَنَا فَذلِكَ الْمُسْلِمُ الَّذِى لَهُ ذِمَّةُ اللهِ وَ ذِمَّةُ رَسُولِ اللهِ فَلَا تُخْفِرُوا اللهَ فِى ذِمَّتِهِ .

AL-JABBAAR

The Compeller

Abu Sa'id al-Khudri reported that some women said to the Prophet, "The men have the advantage of approaching you for knowledge." The Prophet then set aside a day to give the women teachings.

[Transmitted by Bukhari]

عَنْ اَبِى سَعِيدٍ الخُدْرِيِّ قَالَ قَالَ
النِّسَاءُ لِلنَّبِيِّ ﷺ غَلَبَنَا عَلَيْكَ
الرِّجَالُ فَاجْعَلْ لَنَا يَوْمًا مِنْ
نَفْسِكَ فَوَعَدَهُنَّ يَوْمًا لَقِيَهُنَّ
فِيهِ فَوَعَظَهُنَّ وَ اَمَرَهُنَّ

AL-MUTAKABBIR

The Majestic

A man from the Ansar said: "O Messenger of Allah! I heard a hadith which pleases me, but I cannot retain it in my memory." The Messenger of Allah making a sign with his hand for writing said: "Seek the help of your right hand."

[Reported by Abu Hurairah]
[Transmitted by Tirmizi]

عَنْ اَبِي هُرَيْرَةَ قَالَ رَجُلٌ مِنَ الْاَنْصَارِ . . . يَا رَسُولَ اللهِ اِنَّ لَاَسْمَعُ مِنْكَ الْحَدِيثَ فَيُعْجِبُنِي وَلَا اَحْفَظُهُ فَقَالَ رَسُولُ اللهِ عَلَيْهِ اسْتَعِنْ بِيَمِينِكَ وَ اَوْمَأَ بِيَدِهِ الْخَطَّ.

Note: The Ansar were the people in Medina who aided those who fled from Mecca to Medina in the faith of Allah.

AL-KHAALIQ

The Creator

THE MESSENGER OF ALLAH, [peace and blessings of Allah be on him,] has said: "The prophets leave knowledge as their inheritance. The learned ones inherit this great fortune."

[Transmitted by Bukhari]

AL-BAARI

The Evolver

THE MESSENGER OF ALLAH, ^{peace and blessings of Allah be on him,} has said: "Anyone who has nothing of the Qur'an within him is like a ruined house."

[Reported by Ibn Abbas]
[Transmitted by Tirmizi]

عَنِ ابْنِ عَبَّاسٍ قَالَ فَالَ رَسُولُ اللهِ صلى الله عليه وسلم اِنَّ الَّذِى لَيْسَ فِي جَوْفِهِ شَىْءٌ مِنَ الْقُرْآنِ كَالْبَيْتِ الْخَرِبِ.

AL-MUSAWWIR

The Fashioner

THE MESSENGER OF ALLAH, peace and blessings of Allah be on him, has said: "Search Knowlege though it be in China."

[Reported by Anas]
[Transmitted by Ahmad]

Note: Let no distance be too great in the search for knowledge.

عَنْ اَنَسٍ قَالَ قَالَ رَسُولُ اللهِ صَلَّى اللهُ عَلَيْهِ وَسَلَّمَ اُطْلُبُوا الْعِلْمَ وَ لَوْ كَانَ بِالصِّينِ.

AL-GHAFFAAR

The Forgiver

THE MESSENGER OF ALLAH, peace and blessings of Allah be on him, has said: ''The most correct dreams are during the latter part of the night.''

[Reported by Abu Sa'id]
[Transmitted by Bukhari]

عَنْ أَبِى سَعِيدٍ عَنِ النَّبِيِّ صلى الله عليه وسلم قَالَ أَصْدَقُ الرُّؤْيَا بِالسَّحَارِ.

AL-QAHHAAR

The Subduer

A man asked 'Abd-Allah ibn Zaid to show him how the Messenger of Allah performed ablution. "He poured water over his hands washing them twice, rinsed his mouth, sniffed water into his nose three times, washed his face three times, his hands up to the elbows twice, then he wiped his head with both hands, beginning at the forehead and back to the neck, then he washed his feet."

[Reported by Yahya al-Mazini]
[Transmitted by Bukhari]

عَنْ يَحْيَى المازِنِيّ أَنَّ رَجُلاً قَالَ
لِعَبْدِ اللهِ بْنِ زَيْدٍ اَتَسْتَطِيعُ أَنْ
تُرِيَنِي كَيْفَ كَانَ رَسُولُ اللهِ صلى الله عليه وسلم
يَتَوَضَّأُ فَقَالَ عَبْدُ اللهِ بْنُ زَيْدٍ نَعَمْ
فَدَعَا بِمَاءٍ فَأَفْرَغَ عَلَى يَدَيْهِ فَغَسَلَ
يَدَيْهِ مَرَّتَيْنِ ثُمَّ مَضْمَضَ وَ اسْتَنْثَرَ
ثَلاثًا ثُمَّ غَسَلَ وَجْهَهُ ثَلاثًا ثُمَّ غَسَلَ
يَدَيْهِ مَرَّتَيْنِ إِلَى المِرْفَقَيْنِ ثُمَّ مَسَحَ
رَأْسَهُ بِيَدَيْهِ فَأَقْبَلَ بِهِمَا وَ أَدْبَرَ بَدَأَ
بِمُقَدَّمِ رَأْسِهِ حَتَّى ذَهَبَ بِهِمَا إِلَى
قَفَاهُ ثُمَّ رَدَّهَا إِلَى المَكَانِ الَّذِي بَدَأَ
مِنْهُ ثُمَّ غَسَلَ رِجْلَيْهِ .

33

AL-WAHHAAB

The Bestower

THE MESSENGER OF ALLAH, ^{peace and blessings of Allah be on him,} has said: "There is no disease for which Allah has not sent a cure."

[Reported by Abu Hurairah]
[Transmitted by Bukhari]

عَنْ اَبِى هُرَيْرَةَ قَالَ قَالَ رَسُولُ اللهِ صلى الله عليه وسلم مَا اَنْزَلَ اللهُ دَاءً اِلاَّ اَنْزَلَ لَهُ شِفَاءً.

AR-RAZZAAQ

The Provider

THE MESSENGER OF ALLAH, peace and blessings of Allah be on him, has said: "Whoever builds a mosque, desiring Allah's pleasure, Allah builds for him the like of it in paradise.

[Reported by Uthman]
[Transmitted by Bukhari]

عَنْ عُثْمَانَ .... مَنْ بَنَى
مَسْجِدًا .... يَبْتَغِى بِهِ وَجْهَ اللهِ
بَنَى اللهُ لَهُ مِثْلَهُ فِى الْجَنَّةِ.

AL-FATTAAH

The Opener

THE MESSENGER OF ALLAH, ^{peace and blessings of Allah be on him,} has said: "Say part of your prayers at home so your houses do not become like graves."

[Reported by Ibn'Umar]
[Transmitted by Bukhari]

Note: The performing of prayers in a graveyard is not allowed in Islam.

عَنِ ابْنِ عُمَرَ عَنِ النَّبِيِّ صَلَّى اللهُ عَلَيْهِ وَسَلَّمَ قَالَ
اجْعَلُوا فِي بُيُوتِكُمْ مِنْ صَلَاتِكُمْ وَلَا
تَتَّخِذُوهَا قُبُورًا .

AL-ALEEM

The All-Knowing

THE MESSENGER OF ALLAH, peace and blessings of Allah be on him, has said: "The whole earth is a mosque except a graveyard and a bathroom."

[Reported by Abu Sa'id]
[Transmitted by Tirmizi]

عَنْ اَبِى سَعِيدٍ قَالَ قَالَ رَسُولُ اللهِ صلى الله عليه وسلم الْاَرْضُ كُلُّهَا مَسْجِدٌ اِلاَّ الْمَقْبَرَةُ وَ الْحَمَّامُ.

AL-QAABID

The Constrictor

THE MESSENGER OF ALLAH, ^{peace and blessings of Allah be on him,} has said: "When you hear the adhan, say what the mua'dhdhin says."

[Reported by Abu Sa'id al-Khudri]
[Transmitted by Bukhari]

Note: Adhan is the call to prayer sung out by the mua'dhdhin from the minaret of the mosque.

عَنْ اَبِى سَعِيدٍ الخُدْرِىِّ اَنَّ رَسُولَ اللهِ صلى الله عليه وسلم قَالَ اِذَا سَمِعْتُمُ النِّدَاءَ فَقُولُوا مِثْلَ مَا يَقُولُ المُؤَذِّنُ.

AL-BAASIT

The Expander

Abu Mas'ud said, "The Messenger of Allah touched our shoulders at the time of prayer and said, 'Keep straight lines. If you are uneven your hearts will disagree'."

[Transmitted by Muslim]

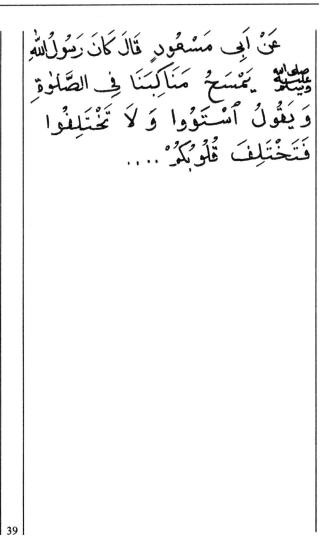

AL-KHAAFID

The Abaser

THE MESSENGER OF ALLAH, peace and blessings of Allah be on him, has said: "Tell me if there is a stream at the door of your house and you bathe in it five times each day, will it leave any dirt?"
They said it would not leave any dirt.
He said: "This is the same as the five prayers with which Allah blots out all faults."

[Reported by Abu Hurairah]
[Transmitted by Bukhari]

Note: The prayers aim at cleaning one's spirit.

عَنْ اَبِى هُرَيْرَةَ اَنَّهُ سَمِعَ رَسُولَ اللهِ ﷺ يَقُولُ اَرَاَيْتُمْ لَوْ اَنَّ نَهْرًا بِبَابِ اَحَدِكُمْ يَغْتَسِلُ فِيهِ كُلَّ يَوْمٍ خَمْسًا مَا تَقُولُ ذَلِكَ يُبْقِى مِنْ دَرَنِهِ قَالُوا لَا يُبْقِى مِنْ دَرَنِهِ شَيْئًا قَالَ فَذَلِكَ مَثَلُ الصَّلَوَاتِ الْخَمْسِ يَمْحُو اللهُ بِهَا الْخَطَايَا .

AR-RAAFE

The Exalter

THE MESSENGER OF ALLAH, _{peace and blessings of Allah be on him,} has said: "When one of you says prayers, he holds a confidence with his Lord."

[Reported by Anas]
[Transmitted by Bukhari]

عَنْ آنَسٍ قَالَ النَّبِي صلى الله عليه وسلم اِنَّ اَحَدَكُمْ اِذَا صَلَّى يُنَاجِى رَبَّهُ .

Note: When he is praying a man should feel that he is alone with his Lord and should open his mind and his heart.

AL-MUIZZ

The Honorer

THE MESSENGER OF ALLAH, ^{peace and blessings of Allah be on him,} has said: "An hour's meditation is better than a year's (unmindful) adoration."

[Reported by Abu Hurairah]
[Transmitted by Ibn Habban]

Note: Meditation on the work of Allah and how to serve humanity best according to the way of Allah.

عَنْ اَبِي هُرَيْرَةَ قَالَ قَالَ رَسُولُ اللهِ صلى الله عليه وسلم تَفَكُّرُ سَاعَةٍ خَيْرٌ مِنْ عِبَادَةِ سَنَةٍ.

AL-MUZILL

The Dishonorer

Abu Qatadah reported that, "While we were praying with the Prophet, he heard the noise of people running. After the prayer he asked the reason for the noise. They said that they were hurrying to prayer. He said, 'Do not hasten but come calmly to prayer'."

[Transmitted by Bukhari]

Note: This does not mean not to come quickly to prayer but to come silently so as not to disturb those praying.

عَنْ اَبِى قَتَادَةَ قَالَ بَيْنَمَا نَحْنُ نُصَلِّى مَعَ النَّبِىِّ صلى الله عليه وسلم اِذْ سَمِعَ جَلَبَةَ رِجَالٍ فَلَمَّا صَلَّى قَالَ مَا شَأْنُكُمْ قَالُوا اسْتَعْجَلْنَا اِلَى الصَّلوةِ . قَالَ فَلَا تَفْعَلُوا اِذَا اَتَيْتُمُ الصَّلوةَ فَعَلَيْكُمُ السَّكِينَةُ فَمَا اَدْرَكْتُمْ فَصَلُّوا مَا فَاتَكُمْ فَاَتِمُّوا.

AS-SAMI'I

The All-Hearing

THE MESSENGER OF ALLAH, peace and blessings of Allah be on him, has said: "There is no prayer for him who does not recite the Opening chapter of the Book."

[Reported by Ubadah]
[Transmitted by Bukhari]

Note: The Fatihah is the opening chapter of the Qur'an.

عَنْ عُبَادَةَ اَنَّ رَسُولَ صلى الله عليه وسلم قَالَ لَا صَلوةَ لِمَنْ لَمْ يَقْرَأْ بِفَاتِحَةِ الْكِتَابِ.

AL-BASEER

The All-Seeing

One day we were praying behind the Prophet. As he raised his head from bowing, he said, ''Allah listens to him who praises Him.'' A man behind him said, ''Our Lord! Yours is the abundant and most excellent praise.''

At the prayer's conclusion he asked, ''Who spoke these words? I saw over thirty angels hastening to be the first to write them.''

[Reported by Rifa'ah]
[Transmitted by Bukhari]

Note: This does not mean that one can utter similar phrases aloud. This was approved by the Prophet himself which is hadith. One may adopt silent expression toward Allah.

عَنْ رِفَاعَةَ قَالَ كُنَّا يَوْمًا نُصَلِّى وَرَاءَ النَّبِيِّ ﷺ فَلَمَّا رَفَعَ رَأْسَهُ مِنَ الرَّكْعَةِ قَالَ سَمِعَ اللهُ لِمَنْ حَمِدَهُ قَالَ رَجُلٌ وَرَاءَهُ رَبَّنَا وَ لَكَ الْحَمْدُ حَمْدًا كَثِيرًا طَيِّبًا مُبَارَكًا فِيهِ فَلَمَّا انْصَرَفَ قَالَ مَنِ الْمُتَكَلِّمُ قَالَ أَنَا قَالَ رَأَيْتُ بِضْعَةً وَثَلَثِينَ مَلَكًا يَبْتَدِرُونَهَا أَيُّهُمْ يَكْتُبُهَا أَوَّلُ.

45

'Isha (early night)
prayer at the Cerrahi
Tekke in Istanbul.

Zuhr (early afternoon) prayer in the Great Mosque in Bursa, Turkey.

Example of the beautiful calligraphy in the Great Mosque in Bursa, Turkey.
preceding page

Muslim who is a cobbler in Konya, Turkey. The joy of one who invokes his Lord is on his face. Wearing two sweaters under his jacket to keep out the winter cold, he works in his little shop which is filled with the light of his being.

A ninety year old Muslim woman whose presence shows the beauty of a being who loves Allah and His Messenger.

AL-HAKAM

The Judge

THE MESSENGER OF ALLAH, ^{peace and blessings of Allah be on him,} has said: "The first thing we do on our day (Id al-Adzha) is to say prayers, then we return and sacrifice an animal. Whoever does this abides by our way."

[Reported by Bara]
[Transmitted by Bukhari]

Note: Id al-Adzha is the feast day when Muslims who can afford to, sacrifice an animal. It is the ninth day of the last lunar month.

عَنِ الْبَرَاءِ قَالَ سَمِعْتُ النَّبِيَّ
صلى الله عليه وسلم يَخْطُبُ فَقَالَ إِنَّ أَوَّلَ مَا نَبْدَأُ
مِنْ يَوْمِنَا هَذَا أَنْ نُصَلِّيَ ثُمَّ نَرْجِعَ
فَنَنْحَرَ فَمَنْ فَعَلَ فَقَدْ أَصَابَ
سُنَّتَنَا.

AL-ADL

The Just

THE MESSENGER OF ALLAH, peace and blessings of Allah be on him, has said: "Our lord, blessed and exalted is He, descends to the nearest part of heaven during the latter third of every night and asks, 'Is there anyone who calls upon Me so I may accept him, does anyone ask of Me so I may grant him, does anyone seek forgiveness of Me so that I may forgive him?'"

[Reported by Abu Hurairah]

[Transmitted by Bukhari]

Note: Descends metaphorically not physically.

عَنْ اَبِى هُرَيْرَةَ اَنَّ رَسُولَ اللهِ صلى الله عليه وسلم قَالَ يَنْزِلُ رَبُّنَا تَبَارَكَ وَ تَعَالَى كُلَّ لَيْلَةٍ اِلَى السَّمَاءِ الدُّنْيَا حِينَ يَبْقَى ثُلُثُ اللَّيْلِ الآخِرُ يَقُولُ مَنْ يَدْعُونِى فَاسْتَجِيبَ لَهُ مَنْ يَسْأَلُنِى فَاُعْطِيَهُ مَنْ يَسْتَغْفِرُنِى فَاغْفِرَ لَهُ.

AL-LATEEF

The Subtle

A'ishah said that the Messenger of Allah kissed Uthman ibn Maz'un while he was dead, and he wept, so that the tears of the Prophet flowed over the face of Uthman.

[Transmitted by Tirmizi]

Note: Uthman ibn Maz'un was the first person to die from among those who fled from Mecca to Medina for the sake of their faith in Allah and belief in the Prophet.

عَنْ عَائِشَةَ قَالَتْ اِنَّ رَسُولَ اللهِ صلى الله عليه وسلم قَبَّلَ عُثْمَانَ ابْنَ مَظْعُونٍ وَهُوَ مَيِّتٌ وَهُوَ يَبْكِي حَتَّى سَالَ دُمُوعُ النَّبِيِّ صلى الله عليه وسلم عَلَى وَجْهِ عُثْمَانَ.

AL-KHABEER

The Aware

THE MESSENGER OF ALLAH, ^{peace and blessings of Allah be on him,} has said: ''Repeat to a dying person, There is no god but Allah.''

[Reported by Abu Sa'id and Abu Hurairah]
[Transmitted by Muslim]

Note: Since the hearing of a person is last to go, this repetition should be repeated as the person is dying and just after death.

عَنْ اَبِى سَعِيدٍ وَ اَبِى هُرَيْرَةَ
قَالَ قَالَ رَسُولُ اللّٰهِ ﷺ لَقِّنُوا مَوْتَاكُمْ
لَا اِلٰهَ اِلَّا اللّٰهُ .

AL-HALEEM

The Clement

THE MESSENGER OF ALLAH, ^{peace and blessings of Allah be on him,} has said: "If a person's last words are 'There is no god but, Allah,' he will enter Paradise."

[Reported by Mu'az ibn Jabal]

[Transmitted by Abu Da'ud]

Note: What is necessary is to live the meaning of these words. This hadith is not to be taken as a permission to do whatever you like in life and at the last moment before dying utter these words.

عَنْ مُعَاذِ بْنِ جَبَلٍ قَالَ قَالَ
رَسُولُ اللهِ صلى الله عليه وسلم مَنْ كَانَ آخِرُ كَلَامِهِ
لَا اِلهَ اِلَّا اللهُ دَخَلَ الْجَنَّةَ.

AL-AZEEM

The Magnificient

Buraidah reported that the Messenger of Allah taught them to say the following at graves: ''Peace be with you, dwellers of this abode, from among the faithful, and we, if Allah wishes, will join you; we ask security for ourselves and for you from Allah.''

[Transmitted by Muslim]

عَنْ بُرَيْدَةَ قَالَ كَانَ رَسُولُ اللهِ صلى الله عليه وسلم يُعَلِّمُهُمْ إِذَا خَرَجُوا إِلَى الْمَقَابِرِ السَّلَامُ عَلَيْكُمْ أَهْلَ الدِّيَارِ مِنَ الْمُؤْمِنِينَ وَ الْمُسْلِمِينَ وَ إِنَّا إِنْ شَاءَ اللهُ بِكُمْ لَلَاحِقُونَ نَسْأَلُ اللهَ لَنَا وَ لَكُمُ الْعَافِيَةَ .

AL-GHAFOOR

The Forgiving

THE MESSENGER OF ALLAH, ^{peace and blessings} has said: "Charity is incumbent on each person every day. Charity is assisting anyone, lifting provisions, saying a good word, every step one takes walking to prayer is charity; showing the way is charity."

[Reported by Abu Hurairah]

[Transmitted by Bukhari]

عَنْ اَبِى هُرَيْرَةَ عَنِ النَّبِى صلى الله عليه وسلم قَالَ كُلُّ سُلَامَى عَلَيْهِ صَدَقَةٌ كُلَّ يَوْمٍ يُعِينُ الرَّجُلَ فِى دَابَّتِهِ يُحَامِلُهُ عَلَيْهَا اَوْ يَرْفَعُ عَلَيْهَا مَنَاعَهُ صَدَقَةٌ وَ الْكَلِمَةُ الطَّيِّبَةُ وَ كُلُّ خُطْوَةٍ يَمْشِيهَا اِلَى الصَّلٰوةِ صَدَقَةٌ وَ دَلُّ الطَّرِيقِ صَدَقَةٌ ؞

ASH-SHAKOOR

The Appreciative

THE MESSENGER OF ALLAH, peace and blessings of Allah be on him, has said: "Removal from the way of that which is harmful is charity."

[Reported by Abu Hurairah]
[Transmitted by Bukhari]

Note: This applies not only to physical obstacles but to any actions which might be harmful to mankind.

عَنْ اَبِى هُرَيْرَةَ عَنِ النَّبِى صلى اﷲ عليه وسلم يُمِيطُ الاَذَى عَنِ الطَّرِيقِ صَدَقَةٌ

AL-ALEE

The Most High

THE MESSENGER OF ALLAH, ^{peace and blessings of Allah be on him,} has said: "Every good deed is charity, and it is a good deed to meet your brother with a cheerful countenance and share with others."

[Reported by Jabir]
[Transmitted by Ahmad]

عَنْ جَابِرٍ قَالَ قَالَ رَسُولُ صلى الله عليه وسلم
كُلُّ مَعْرُوفٍ صَدَقَةٌ وَ إِنَّ
مِنَ المَعْرُوفِ أَنْ تَلْقَى أَخَاكَ
بِوَجْهٍ طَلْقٍ وَ أَنْ تُفْرِغَ مِنْ
دَلْوِكَ فِي إِنَاءِ أَخِيكَ .

AL-KABEER

The Great

THE MESSENGER OF ALLAH, ^{peace and blessings of Allah be on him,} has said: "A prostitute saw a dog panting, dying of thirst, on top of a well. She removed her boot, tied it to her head covering and drew water for the dog. She was forgiven on this account."

[Reported by Abu Hurairah]
[Transmitted by Bukhari and Muslim]

Note: Dhunnuni Misri (a saint), while travelling to Mecca for the seventieth time, came across a dog panting from thirst. As he had no provisions for hajj he offered the reward of all his pilgrimages to anyone who would give the dog water.

عَنْ اَبِى هُرَيْرَةَ قَالَ قَالَ رَسُولُ اللهِ صلى الله عليه وسلم غُفِرَ لِاِمْرَاَةٍ مُومِسَةٍ مَرَّتْ بِكَلْبٍ عَلَى رَأْسٍ رَكِيٍّ يَلْهَثُ كَادَ يَقْتُلُهُ العَطَشُ فَنَزَعَتْ خُفَّهَا فَاَوْثَقَتْهُ بِخِمَارِهَا فَنَزَعَتْ لَهُ مِنَ المَاءِ فَغُفِرَ لَهَا بِذٰلِكَ ....

AL-HAFEEZ

The Preserver

THE MESSENGER OF ALLAH, ^{peace and blessings of Allah be on him,} has said: "There is a man who conceals his charity so well that his left hand does not know what his right hand gives."

[Reported by Abu Hurairah]
[Transmitted by Bukhari]

Note: A reason for secret charity is to perform a deed only for the sake of Allah, wanting no earthly reward. Another reason is not to offend the person receiving the charity.

قَالَ اَبُو هُرَيْرَة عَنِ النَّبِيِّ صَلَّى اللهُ عَلَيْهِ وَسَلَّمَ

وَ رَجُلٌ تَصَدَّقَ بِصَدَقَةٍ فَاَخْفَاهَا

حَتَّى لَا تَعْلَمَ شِمَالُهُ مَا تُنْفِقُ

يَمِينُهُ

AL-MUQEET

The Sustainer

THE MESSENGER OF ALLAH, peace and blessings of Allah be on him, has said: "He who is devoid of kindness is devoid of good."

[Reported by Jarir]
[Transmitted by Muslim]

عَنْ جَرِيرٍ عَنِ النَّبِيِّ صلى الله عليه وسلم قَالَ
مَنْ يُحْرَمُ الرِّفْقَ يُحْرَمُ الخَيْرَ.

AL-HASEEB

The Reckoner

THE MESSENGER OF ALLAH, ^{peace and blessings of Allah be on him,} has said: "Fasting is an armor with which one protects oneself. The person who fasts should not speak lies or curse another. The odor of the mouth of one fasting is sweeter to Allah than the oder of musk."

[Reported by Abu Hurairah]
[Transmitted by Bukhari]

Note: While fasting, a believer must be more careful not to lie, which is why the odor from the mouth of one fasting is regarded sweeter to Allah.

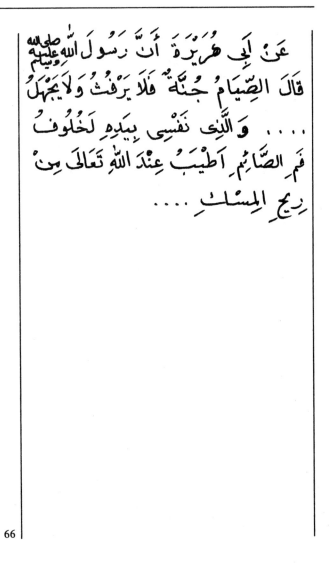

AL-JALEEL

The Sublime

THE MESSENGER OF ALLAH, peace and blessings of Allah be on him, has said: "He who does not give up uttering lies and acting according to them, Allah has no need of his giving up food and drink."

[Reported by Abu Hurairah]

[Transmitted by Bukhari]

عَنْ اَبِي هُرَيْرَةَ قَالَ قَالَ رَسُولُ اللهِ صلى الله عليه وسلم مَنْ لَمْ يَدَعْ قَوْلَ الزُّورِ وَ العَمَلَ بِهِ فَلَيْسَ لِلهِ حَاجَةٌ فِي اَنْ يَدَعَ طَعَامَهُ وَ شَرَابَهُ.

AL-KAREEM

The Generous

Anas said, ''We used to journey with the Prophet, and he who kept the fast found no fault with him who broke it, nor did he who broke the fast find fault with him who kept it.''

[Transmitted by Bukhari]

AR-RAQEEB

The Watchful

THE MESSENGER OF ALLAH, peace and blessings of Allah be on him, has said: "When one forgets and eats or drinks, he should complete his fast, for Allah made him eat and drink."

[Reported by Abu Hurairah]
[Transmitted by Bukhari]

AL-MUJEEB

The Responsive

Abdullah ibn Mas'ud reported that the Messenger of Allah fasted the first three days of every month and rarely broke fast on Friday.

[Transmitted by Tirmizi]

Note: This fast is other than the fast of Ramadan and refers to the lunar calendar which would put the days of fasting on the 13th, 14th, and 15th. He only fasted on Friday when it fell on one of these three days because for the Muslim, Friday is regarded as a feast day.

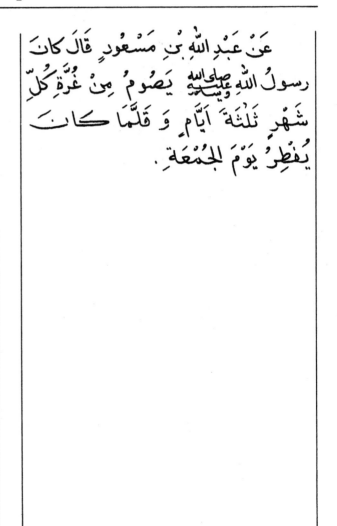

AL-WAASI

The All-Embracing

THE MESSENGER OF ALLAH, peace and blessings of Allah be on him, has said: "There is zakat (charity) for everything, and the zakat for the body is fasting."

[Reported by Abu Hurairah]
[Transmitted by Ibn Majah]

عَنْ اَبِي هُرَيْرَةَ قَالَ قَالَ رَسُولُ اللهِ صلى الله عليه وسلم لِكُلِّ شَيْءٍ زَكَوةٌ وَ زَكَوةُ لِلْجَسَدِ الصَّوْمُ.

71

AL-HAKEEM

The Wise

THE MESSENGER OF ALLAH, peace and blessings of Allah be on him, has said: "He who serves the merciful, gives food and gives greeting (from his heart), will enter Paradise with peace."

[Reported by Abdullah ibn 'Amr]
[Transmitted by Tirmizi]

Note: The Muslim places his right hand on his heart indicating that the five pillars of Islam are in his heart and that no harm will come from him.

عَنْ عَبْدِ اللهِ بْنِ عَمْرٍو قَالَ قَالَ رَسُولُ اللهِ صلى الله عليه وسلم اُعْبُدُوا الرَّحْمٰنَ وَ اَطْعِمُوا الطَّعَامَ وَ اَفْشُوا السَّلَامَ تَدْخُلُوا الْجَنَّةَ بِسَلَامٍ.

AL-WADOOD

The Loving

Ibn 'Abbas said: "The people of Yaman used to go to pilgrimage with no provisions." They said: "We trust in Allah." When they came to Mecca they begged from others, so Allah revealed: "And make provision, for the benefit of provision is the guarding of oneself."

[Transmitted by Bukhari]

عَنِ ابْنِ عَبَّاسٍ قَالَ كَانَ أَهْلُ الْيَمَنِ يَحُجُّونَ وَ لَا يَتَزَوَّدُونَ وَ يَقُولُونَ نَحْنُ الْمُتَوَكِّلُونَ فَإِذَا قَدِمُوا مَكَّةَ سَأَلُوا النَّاسَ فَأَنْزَلَ اللهُ عَزَّ وَجَلَّ وَ تَزَوَّدُوا فَإِنَّ خَيْرَ الزَّادِ التَّقْوَى .

The place of khalwat
(retreat) of a Shaikh in
Istanbul. It is below
ground level and
cantilevered over water.
There is one entrance
and one laticed window
for air. Here the dervish
doe's salat (prayers) and
dhikr. He has prepared
for his personal dhikr by
the many hours of
repetition done in the
dhikr circle.

Detail of ceiling in the
Hagia Sophia Mosque,
Istanbul, Turkey. There
was a time when 10,000
men formed the circle of
dhikr here.

Hattat Hamid al-Amidi writing Ah! Tesslimiyet, in his small room which suffers from a leaky ceiling, no heat and no plumbing. In the midst of these conditions Hamid, in his overcoat, writes the Beautiful Names of Allah.

Shadhili Tekke of Shaikh Zafir, Istanbul, Turkey.

*The dervish is like a pot
full of food which must
be emptied each day.*

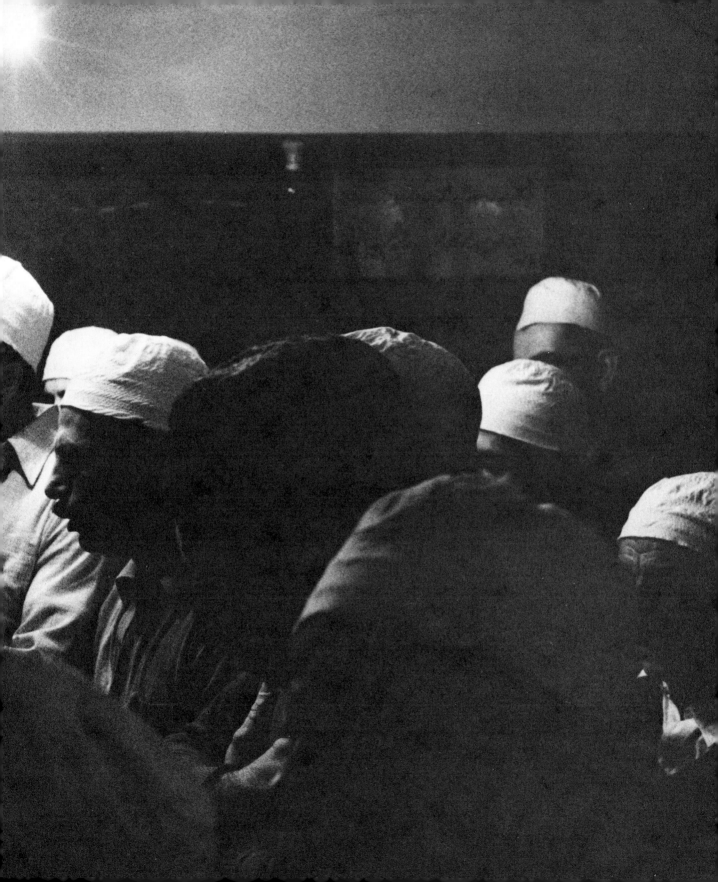

Muslim women and their daughters preparing a meal in a tekke.

*Dervish brothers share
a meal in the Muslim
tradition.*

Minaret of an old Mosque in Istanbul.

Detail of the Blue Mosque in Istanbul showing a minaret.

Looking through a window of a tekke in Istanbul where two Shaikhs are buried.

AL-MAJEED

The Glorious

Ibn 'Umar reported, ''The saying of labbaika by the Messenger of Allah was this: I am at Your service, O Allah! I am at Your service. I am at Your service, there is none like You, I am at Your service.

Yours is the praise, the blessing and the kingdom, there is none like You.''

[Transmitted by Bukhari]

عَنِ ابْنِ عُمَرَ أَنَّ تَلْبِيَةَ رَسُولِ اللهِ صلى الله عليه وسلم لَبَّيْكَ اللّهُمَّ لَبَّيْكَ لَبَّيْكَ لَا شَرِيكَ لَكَ لَبَّيْكَ إِنَّ الْحَمْدَ وَ النِّعْمَةَ لَكَ وَ الْمُلْكُ لَكَ لَا شَرِيكَ لَكَ .

AL-BAA'ITH

The Resurrector

Abu Sa'id al Khudri reported that the Messenger of Allah was asked, ''Who is the most excellent of men?''
The Messenger of Allah said, ''The believer who strives hard in the way of Allah with both his person and his property.''

[Transmitted by Bukhari]

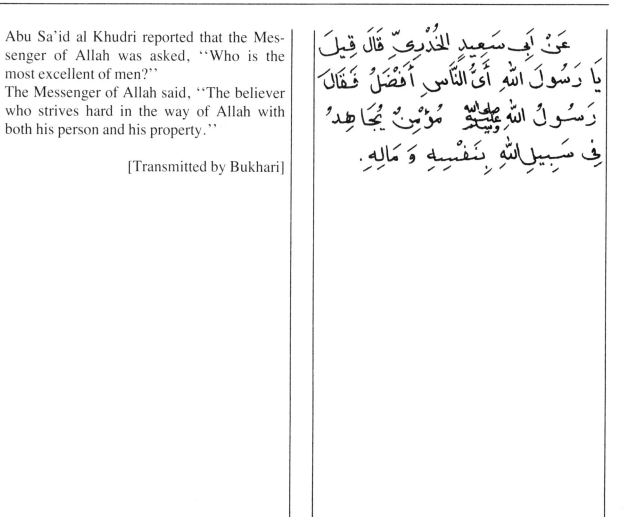

ASH-SHAHEED

The Witness

A woman was found among the dead in one of the battles, so the Messenger of Allah forbade the killing of women and children.

[Reported by Abdullah]
[Transmitted by Bukhari]

عَنْ عَبْدِ اللهِ اَنَّ اَمْرَأَةً وُجِدَتْ فِي بَعْضِ مَغَازِى النَّبِي صلى الله عليه وسلم مَقْتُولَةً فَاَنْكَرَ رَسُولُ اللهِ صلى الله عليه وسلم قَتْلَ النِّسَاءِ وَ الصِّبْيَانِ .

AL-HAQQ

The Truth

THE MESSENGER OF ALLAH, _{peace and blessings of Allah be on him,} has said: "Marriage is incumbent on all who possess the ability, it keeps the eye cast down and keeps a man chaste; he who cannot, should take to fasting which will cool his passion."

[Reported by Alqamah]

[Transmitted by Bukhari]

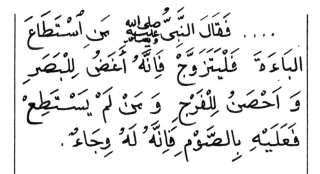

AL-WAKEEL

The Trustee

Abu Rafi said he saw the Messenger of Allah repeat the call for prayer in the ear of Hasan, the son of Ali, when Fatimah gave birth to him.

[Transmitted by Tirmizi]

عَنْ اَبِى رَافِعٍ قَالَ رَأَيْتُ رَسُوْلَ اللهِ صَلَّى اللهُ عَلَيْهِ وَسَلَّمَ اَذَّنَ فِى اُذُنِ الْحَسَنِ بْنِ عَلِيٍّ حِيْنَ وَلَدَتْهُ فَاطِمَةُ بِالصَّلٰوةِ.

AL-QAWEE

The Strong

THE MESSENGER OF ALLAH, peace and blessings of Allah be on him, has said: ''The best of you is he who is best to his family; I am the best among you to my family. When your companion dies, leave him.''

[Reported by A'ishah]
[Transmitted by Tirmizi]

Note: This last part means that when someone you know dies, one should not speak ill of him.

عَنْ عَائِشَـةَ قَالَتْ قَالَ
رَسُولُ اللهِ خَيْرُكُمْ خَيْرُكُمْ لِاَهْلِهِ وَاَنَا
خَيْرُكُمْ لِاَهْلِي وَ إِذَا مَاتَ صَاحِبُكُمْ
فَدَعُوهُ .

AL-MATEEN

The Firm

THE MESSENGER OF ALLAH, ^{peace and blessings of Allah be on him,} has said: "Let no believing man hate his believing wife; if he is displeased with one trait of her character, let him be pleased with another that is within her."

[Reported by Abu Hurairah]
[Transmitted by Muslim]

Note: A Muslim is allowed to marry a woman of another religion if that religion is one that has a holy book from God.

عَنْ أَبِي هُرَيْرَةَ قَالَ قَالَ رَسُولُ اللهِ صلى الله عليه وسلم لَا يَفْرُكُ مُؤْمِنٌ مُؤْمِنَةً إِنْ كَرِهَ مِنْهَا خُلُقاً رَضِيَ مِنْهَا آخَرَ

AL-WALEE

The Protecting Friend

THE MESSENGER OF ALLAH, ^{peace and blessings of Allah be on him,} used to take three breaths in a drink. He said that it was highly thirst removing, conducive to health and good for digestion.

[Reported by Anas]
[Transmitted by Muslim]

Note: Drink applies to any non-alcoholic beverage. Alcoholic drinks are forbidden in Islam as mentioned in the Qur'an.

عَنْ اَنَسٍ قَالَ كَانَ رَسُولُ اللهِ صلى الله عليه وسلم يَتَنَفَّسُ فِي الشَّرَابِ ثَلْثًا .... وَ يَقُولُ اِنَّهُ اَرْوَى وَ اَبْرَءُ وَ اَمْرَءُ .

AL-HAMEED

The Praiseworthy

THE MESSENGER OF ALLAH, peace and blessings of Allah be on him, has said: "The food of one is sufficient for two, the food of two is sufficient for four, and the food of four is sufficient for eight."

[Reported by Jabir]
[Transmitted by Muslim]

عَنْ جَابِرٍ قَالَ سَمِعْتُ رَسُولَ اللهِ صلى الله عليه وسلم يَقُولُ طَعَامُ الْوَاحِدِ يَكْفِي الاِثْنَيْنِ وَطَعَامُ الاِثْنَيْنِ يَكْفِي الأَرْبَعَةِ وَطَعَامُ الأَرْبَعَةِ يَكْفِي الثَّمَانِيَةِ .

AL-MUHSEE

The Reckoner

THE MESSENGER OF ALLAH, ^{peace and blessings of Allah be on him,} has said: ''No one eats better food than that which he eats from the work of his own hands.''

[Reported by al-Miqdam]
[Transmitted by Bukhari]

عَنِ المِقْدَامِ عَنْ رَسُولِ اللهِ صَلَى الله عَلَيْهِ وَسَلَّمَ قَالَ مَا أَكَلَ أَحَدٌ طَعَامًا قَطْ خَيْرًا مِنْ أَنْ يَأْكُلَ مِنْ عَمَلِ يَدِهِ.

AL-MUBDI

The Originator

THE MESSENGER OF ALLAH, peace and blessings of Allah be on him, has said: ''No person can drink a better draught than that of anger which he swallows for the sake of Allah.''

[Reported by Ibn 'Umar]
[Transmitted by Ahmad]

عَنِ ابْنِ عُمَرَ قَالَ قَالَ رَسُولُ اللهِ صلى الله عليه وسلم مَا تَجَرَّعَ عَبْدٌ أَفْضَلَ عِنْدَ اللهِ عَزَّوَجَلَّ مِنْ جُرْعَةِ غَيْظٍ يَكْظِمُهَا ابْتِغَاءَ وَجْهِ اللهِ تَعَالَى.

AL-MU'EED

The Restorer

THE MESSENGER OF ALLAH, ^{peace and blessings of Allah be on him,} has said: "Neither merchandise nor selling divert these men from the remembrance of Allah."

[Reported by Qatadah]
[Transmitted by Bukhari]

قَالَ قَتَادَةُ . . . . لَمْ تُلْهِهِمْ تِجَارَةٌ وَ لَا بَيْعٌ عَنْ ذِكْرِ اللهِ حَتَّى يُؤَدُّوهُ اِلَى اللهِ.

AL-MUHYEE

The Giver of Life

THE MESSENGER OF ALLAH, ^{peace and blessings of Allah be on him,} has said: "May Allah have mercy on the man who is generous when he buys, sells, and asks his due."

[Reported by Jabir]
[Transmitted by Bukhari]

عَنْ جَابِرٍ أَنَّ رَسُولَ اللهِ صلى الله عليه وسلم قَالَ رَحِمَ اللهُ رَجُلاً سَمْحًا اِذَا بَاعَ وَ اِذَا اشْتَرَى وَ اِذَا اقْتَضَى .

AL-MUMEET

The Creator of Death

THE MESSENGER OF ALLAH, ^{peace and blessings of Allah be on him,} has said: "Those who keep back grain in order to sell at a high rate are sinners."

[Reported by Ma'mar]
[Transmitted by Muslim]

عَنْ مَعْمَرٍ قَالَ قَالَ رَسُولُ اللهِ صَلَّى اللهُ عَلَيْهِ وَسَلَّمَ مَنِ احْتَكَرَ فَهُوَ خَاطِئٌ

AL-HAYY

The Alive

THE MESSENGER OF ALLAH, peace and blessings of Allah be on him, has said: "It is charity for any Muslim who plants a tree or cultivates land which provides food for a bird, animal, or man."

[Reported by Anas]
[Transmitted by Bukhari]

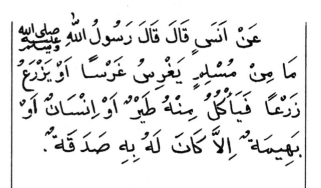

AL-QAYYOOM

The Self-Subsisting

THE MESSENGER OF ALLAH, ^{peace and blessings of Allah be on him,} has said many times in prayers, ''Seek Allah's refuge from sin and being in debt.'' Someone asked the reason for this repetition. He said, ''When a man is in debt he speaks and tells lies; promises and breaks the promise.''

[Reported by A'ishah]
[Transmitted by Bukhari]

عَنْ عَائِشَةَ أَنَّ رَسُولَ اللهِ صلى الله عليه وسلم كَانَ
يَدْعُو فِي الصَّلٰوةِ وَيَقُولُ اللّٰهُمَّ إِنِّي أَعُوذُ
بِكَ مِنَ الْمَأْثَمِ وَ الْمَغْرَمِ فَقَالَ لَهُ قَائِلٌ
مَا أَكْثَرَ مَا تَسْتَعِيذُ يَا رَسُولَ اللهِ
مِنَ الْمَغْرَمِ قَالَ إِنَّ الرَّجُلَ إِذَا غَرِمَ
حَدَّثَ فَكَذِبَ وَ وَعَدَ فَأَخْلَفَ .

AL-WAAJID

The Finder

A'ishah reported that some people asked about eating meat over which they were not certain the name of Allah had been mentioned. The Prophet said: ''Mention the name of Allah over it and eat.'' A'ishah said these people were recent believers.

[Transmitted by Bukhari]

عَنْ عَائِشَةَ أَنَّ قَوْمًا قَالُوا لِلنَّبِيِّ
صلى الله عليه وسلم إِنَّ قَوْمًا يَأْتُونَنَا بِاللَّحْمِ لَا نَدْرِى
أَذُكِرَ اسْمُ اللهِ عَلَيْهِ أَمْ لَا فَقَالَ سَمُّوا
عَلَيْهِ أَنْتُمْ وَ كُلُوهُ قَالَتْ وَكَانُواحَدِيثِى
عَهْدٍ بِالْكُفْرِ .

AL-MAAJID

The Noble

THE MESSENGER OF ALLAH, ^{peace and blessings} ^{of Allah be on him,} has said: "Every drink that intoxicates is prohibited."

[Reported by A'ishah]
[Transmitted by Bukhari]

عَنْ عَائِشَـةَ .... فَقَالَ رَسُولُ اللهِ صلى الله عليه وسلم كُلُّ شَرَابٍ اَسْكَرَ فَهُوَ حَرَامٌ.

AL-WAAHID

The Unique

THE MESSENGER OF ALLAH, peace and blessings of Allah be on him, has said: "The blessing of food is washing hands before and after the meal."

[Reported by Salman]
[Transmitted by Tirmizi]

عَنْ سَلْمَانَ .... فَقَالَ رَسُولُ اللهِ صلى الله عليه وسلم بَرَكَةُ الطَّعَامِ الوُضُوءُ قَبْلَهُ وَ الوُضُوءُ بَعْدَهُ .

AL-AHAD

The One

THE MESSENGER OF ALLAH, peace and blessings of Allah be on him, has said: "Eat together, not separately, for the blessing is to eat with company."

[Reported by 'Umar]
[Transmitted by Ibn Majah]

عَنْ عُمَرَ قَالَ قَالَ رَسُولُ اللهِ صلى الله عليه وسلم كُلُوا جَمِيعًا وَ لَا تَفَرَّقُوا فَإِنَّ البَرَكَةَ مَعَ الجَمَاعَةِ.

AS-SAMAD

The Eternal

THE MESSENGER OF ALLAH, peace and blessings of Allah be on him, saw a man lying on his stomach and said, ''Allah does not like this posture.''

[Reported by Abu Hurairah]
[Transmitted by Tirmizi]

Note: This position of lying is unhealthy for it puts pressure on the stomach which cannot digest properly.

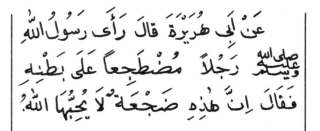

AL-QAADIR

The Able

THE MESSENGER OF ALLAH, ^{peace and blessings of Allah be on him,} has said: "There are two blessings which most people misuse—health and leisure."

[Reported by Abu 'Umar]
[Transmitted by Bukhari]

عَنْ اَبِى عُمَرَ قَالَ قَالَ رَسُولُ اللهِ صلى الله عليه وسلم نِعْمَتَانِ مَغْبُونٌ فِيهِمَا كَثِيرٌ مِنَ النَّاسِ الصِّحَّةُ وَ الْفَرَاغُ.

Note: Another hadith tells of these considerations: health before one may become ill, youth before growing old, prosperity before you may experience poverty, and leisure before a time comes when you have none.

AL-MUQTADIR

The Powerful

THE MESSENGER OF ALLAH, peace and blessings of Allah be on him, has said: "It is the sunnah (what the Prophet did) that a man should accompany his guest to the door of the house."

[Reported by Abu Hurairah]
[Transmitted by Ibn Majah]

عَنْ أَبِى هُرَيْرَةَ قَالَ قَالَ رَسُولُ اللّٰهِ صلى الله عليه وسلم مِنَ السُّنَّةِ أَنْ تَخْرُجَ الرَّجُلُ مَعَ ضَيْفِهِ إِلَى بَابِ الدَّارِ.

AL-MUQADDIM

The Expediter

A'ishah was asked what the Prophet did in his house. She said, "He served his wife," meaning that he did work for his wife.

[Reported by Aswad]
[Transmitted by Bukhari]

عَنِ الأَسْوَدِ قَالَ سَأَلْتُ عَائِشَةَ مَا كَانَ النَّبِيُّ ﷺ يَصْنَعُ فِي بَيْتِهِ قَالَتْ كَانَ يَكُونُ فِي مِهْنَةِ أَهْلِهِ تَعْنِي خِدْمَةَ أَهْلِهِ .

*Muqarnas (stalactites),
on the portal of the
Beyazit Mosque in
Istanbul.
preceding page*

*Interior of a small
mosque in Istanbul
showing the mihrab
(prayer niche), and the
minbar, where the Imam
stands when delivering a
discourse.*

An entrance to the Emir Sultan Mosque in Bursa, Turkey.

AL-MUAKHIR

The Delayer

THE MESSENGER OF ALLAH, peace and blessings of Allah be on him, has said: "Help your brother whether he does wrong or wrong is done to him."
Then the Prophet was asked, "How can we help the wrongdoer?"
He answered: "Take hold of his hands preventing him from doing wrong."

[Reported by Anas]
[Transmitted by Bukhari]

عَنْ اَنَسٍ قَالَ قَالَ رَسُولُ اللهِ صلى الله عليه وسلم اُنْصُرْ اَخَاكَ ظَالِمًا اَوْ مَظْلُومًا قَالُوا يَا رَسُولَ اللهِ هٰذَا نَنْصُرُهُ مَظْلُومًا فَكَيْفَ نَنْصُرُهُ ظَالِمًا قَالَ تَأْخُذُ فَوْقَ يَدَيْهِ .

AL-AWWAL

The First

THE MESSENGER OF ALLAH, peace and blessings of Allah be on him, has said: "You will recognize the faithful, for they show mercy to one another, love one another and are kind to one another as if they all were of the same body. When one member of the body ails, the entire body ails."

[Reported by Nu'man]
[Transmitted by Bukhari]

عَنِ النُّعْمَانِ يَقُولُ قَالَ رَسُولُ اللهِ صلى الله عليه وسلم تَرَى الْمُؤْمِنِينَ فِي تَرَاحُمِهِمْ وَ تَوَادِّهِمْ وَ تَعَاطُفِهِمْ كَمَثَلِ الْجَسَدِ اِذَا اشْتَكَى عُضْوًا تَدَاعَى لَهُ سَائِرُ جَسَدِهِ بِالسَّهَرِ وَ الْحُمَّى .

AL-AAKHIR

The Last

"I served the Prophet for ten years and he never expressed displeasure with me or asked, 'Why did you do this or, Why did you not do this?'"

[Reported by Anas]
[Transmitted by Bukhari]

عَنْ اَنَسٍ قَالَ خَدَمْتُ النَّبِيَّ صلى الله عليه وسلم عَشْرَ سِنِينَ فَمَا قَالَ لِي أُفٍّ وَلاَ لِمَ صَنَعْتَ وَلاَ اَنْ لاَ صَنَعْتَ

AZ-ZAAHIR

The Manifest

THE MESSENGER OF ALLAH, ^{peace and blessings of Allah be on him,} has said: "Whoever believes in Allah and the next world, should not harm his neighbor and should honor his guest."

[Reported by Abu Hurairah]

[Transmitted by Bukhari]

عَنْ اَبِى هُرَيْرَةَ قَالَ قَالَ رَسُولُ اللهِ صَلَّى اللهُ عَلَيْهِ وَسَلَّمَ مَنْ كَانَ يُؤْمِنُ بِاللهِ وَ الْيَوْمِ الْآخِرِ فَلَا يُؤْذِ جَارَهُ وَ مَنْ كَانَ يُؤْمِنُ بِاللهِ وَالْيَوْمِ الْآخِرِ فَلْيَكْرِمْ ضَيْفَهُ.

AL-BAATIN

The Hidden

THE MESSENGER OF ALLAH, peace and blessings of Allah be on him, has said: "The best Islam is that you feed the poor and offer salutations to those you know and those you do not know."

[Reported by Abdullah ibn 'Amr]
[Transmitted by Bukhari]

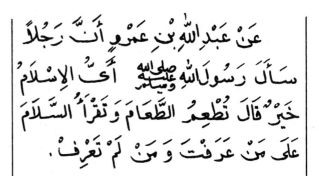

AL-WAALI

The Governor

THE MESSENGER OF ALLAH, ^{peace and blessings of Allah be on him,} has said: "He who keeps silence will be safe."

[Reported by 'Abdullah ibn 'Amr]
[Transmitted by Ahmad and Tirmizi]

Note: A man should not use his tongue to insult others.

عَنْ عَبْدِ اللهِ بْنِ عَمْرٍو قَالَ قَالَ رَسُولُ اللهِ صلى الله عليه وسلم مَنْ صَمَتَ نَجَا.

AL-MUTA'AAL

The Most Exalted

THE MESSENGER OF ALLAH, ^{peace and blessings of Allah be on him,} has said: "When you observe four things there is nothing in the world that may cause your loss of bliss: guarding of a trust, truthfulness in speech, good conduct, and moderation in food, (eating, drinking and living)."

[Reported by Abdullah ibn 'Amr]
[Transmitted by Ahmad]

عَنْ عَبْدِ اللهِ بْنِ عَمْرٍو أَنَّ رَسُولَ
اللهِ ﷺ قَالَ أَرْبَعٌ إِذَا كُنَّ فِيكَ
فَلَا عَلَيْكَ مَا فَاتَكَ الدُّنْيَا حِفْظُ
أَمَانَةٍ وَصِدْقُ حَدِيثٍ وَحُسْنُ خَلِيقَةٍ
وَعِفَّةٌ فِي طُعْمَةٍ .

122

AL-BARR

The Source of All Goodness

THE MESSENGER OF ALLAH, ^{peace and blessings of Allah be on him,} has said: "Allah does not take into account your figures or your wealth, He looks and values your hearts and deeds."

[Reported by Abu Hurairah]

[Transmitted by Muslim]

عَنْ اَبِى هُرَيْرَةَ قَالَ قَالَ رَسُولُ اللهِ صلى الله عليه وسلم اِنَّ اللهَ لَا يَنْظُرُ اِلَى صُوَرِكُمْ وَ اَمْوَالِكُمْ وَ لٰكِنْ يَنْظُرُ اِلَى اَعْمَالِكُمْ

AT-TAWWAAB

The Acceptor of Repentence

THE MESSENGER OF ALLAH, ^{peace and blessings of Allah be on him,} has said: "Give presents to one another; for a present removes hatred."

[Reported by A'ishah]
[Transmitted by Tirmizi]

Note: Another hadith states, "give presents to one another; you will have love for one another."

عَنْ عَائِشَةَ عَنِ النَّبِيِّ صلى الله عليه وسلم قَالَ تَهَادُوا فَإِنَّ الْهَدِيَّةَ تَذْهَبُ الضَّغَائِنَ.

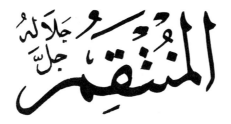

AL-MUNTAQIM

The Avenger

THE MESSENGER OF ALLAH, ^{peace and blessings of Allah be on him,} has said: ''The most pleasing names to Allah are Abdullah (servant of Allah) and Abdur Rahman (servant of the merciful).''

[Reported by Ibn 'Umar]
[Transmitted by Muslim]

Note: This does not mean that these two names should be given to everyone but implies that children should be named with a name that reminds one of Allah.

عَنِ ابْنِ عُمَرَ قَالَ قَالَ رَسُولُ اللهِ صلى الله عليه وسلم اِنَّ اَحَبَّ اَسْمَائِكُمُ اِلَى اللهِ عَبْدُ اللهِ وَ عَبْدُ الرَّحْمٰنِ.

AL-AFUWW

The Pardoner

THE MESSENGER OF ALLAH, _{peace and blessings of Allah be on him,} has said:"This world is a prison for the believer and a paradise for the unbeliever."

[Reported by Abu Hurairah]
[Transmitted by Muslim]

عَنْ اَبِي هُرَيْرَةَ قَالَ قَالَ رَسُولُ اللهِ صَلَّى اللهُ عَلَيْهِ وَسَلَّمَ الدُّنْيَا سِجْنُ الْمُؤْمِنِ وَجَنَّةُ الْكَافِرِ.

AR-RAOOF

The Compassionate

THE PROPHET MUHAMMAD, ^{Peace and blessings of Allah be on him.} slept upon a mat and got up with marks on his body made by the mat. Someone said, "O Messenger of Allah! If you had asked, I would have spread a soft bed for you." The Prophet said: "What business have I with the world? My state in respect to the world is that of a man on horseback who stops under the shade of a tree for awhile and then leaves."

[Reported by Ibn Mas'ud]
[Transmitted by Ahmad and Tirmizi]

عَنِ ابْنِ مَسْعُودٍ اَنَّ رَسُولَ اللهِ صلى الله عليه وسلم نَامَ عَلَى حَصِيرٍ فَقَامَ وَ قَدْ اَثَّرَ فِى جَسَدِهِ فَقَالَ ابْنُ مَسْعُودٍ يَا رَسُولَ اللهِ لَوْ اَمَرْتَنَا اَنْ نَبْسُطَ لَكَ وَ نَعْمَلَ فَقَالَ مَا لِى وَ لِلدُّنْيَا وَ مَا اَنَا وَ الدُّنْيَا اِلاَّ كَرَاكِبٍ اسْتَظَلَّ تَحْتَ شَجَرَةٍ ثُمَّ رَاحَ وَ تَرَكَهَا.

Note: The mat referred to here was woven from the leaves of a date tree. Man should understand that his stay on earth is temporary and should be satisfied with what he has. This does not mean that man should be complacent, but that his desire for more should not overtake his entire life. There is a hadith which says a man should work as if he will never die and he should also pray as if he were to die tomorrow.

MAALIK-UL-MULK

The Owner of Sovereignty

THE MESSENGER OF ALLAH, ^{peace and blessings of Allah be on him,} has said: "There is a calamity for every people, and the calamity for my people is wealth."

[Reported by Ka'b ibn 'Iyad]
[Transmitted by Tirmizi]

Note: *My people* refers to *ummat of Muhammad* in the Arabic text which means those who have embraced Islam.

عَنْ كَعْبِ بْنِ عِيَاضٍ قَالَ سَمِعْتُ
رَسُولَ اللهِ صلى الله عليه وسلم يَقُولُ اِنَّ لِكُلِّ اُمَّةٍ
فِتْنَةٌ وَ فِتْنَةُ اُمَّتِى الْمَالُ.

ZUL-JALAALI-WAL-IKRAAM

The Lord of Majesty and Bounty

THE MESSENGER OF ALLAH, ^{peace and blessings of Allah be on him,} A man came to the Messenger of Allah and asked for an injunction and for it to be brief. He said, ''When you stand up to pray perform your prayer as if it were your last. Do not say anything you will have to make excuses for tomorrow and resolve to give up all hopes of what men possess.''

[Reported by Abu Ayyub al-Ansari]
[Transmitted by Ahmad]

عَنْ اَبِى اَيُّوبَ الْاَنْصَارِىِّ قَالَ جَاءَ
رَجُلٌ اِلَى النَّبِىِّ صَلَّى اللهُ وَسَلَّمَ فَقَالَ عِظْنِى وَاَوْجِزْ
فَقَالَ اِذَا قُمْتَ فِى صَلَاتِكَ فَصَلِّ صَلوةَ
مُوَدِّعٍ وَ لَا تَكَلَّمْ بِكَلَامٍ تَعْذِرُ مِنْهُ غَدًا
وَ اَجْمِعْ الْاِيَاسَ مِمَّا فِى يَدَىِ النَّاسِ.

AL-MUQSIT

The Equitable

THE MESSENGER OF ALLAH, _{peace and blessings of Allah be on him,} has said: "The parable of my people is that of rain. It is not known whether its beginning is better than its end."

[Reported by Ja'far]
[Transmitted by Razin]

Note: *My people* refers to those who saw Muhammad and believed in him, those who did not see him and believed in him, and those who will come to this world and believe in him.

This shows that there will be people of the ummat who live after the Prophet and will serve Islam during a critical time, and these people may be looked upon as being more important than some of those who lived during the Prophet's lifetime.

عَنْ جَعْفَرٍ عَنْ اَبِيهِ عَنْ جَدِّهِ قَالَ قَالَ رَسُولُ اللهِ ﷺ . . . . مَثَلُ اُمَّتِي مَثَلُ الغَيْثِ لاَ يُدْرَكُ اٰخِرُهُ خَيْرٌ اَمْ اَوَّلُهُ .

AL-JAAME'

The Gatherer

THE MESSENGER OF ALLAH, ^{peace and blessings of Allah be on him,} has said: ''Virtue is good conduct and vice is thoughts which if known by others would be shameful.''

[Reported by An-Nawas ibn Sam'an]
[Transmitted by Muslim]

Note: Good conduct is the first step toward virtue which is Allah's reward for living according to His laws.

عَنِ النَّوَّاسِ بنِ سَمْعَانَ قَالَ سَأَلْتُ رَسُولَ اللهِ صلى الله عليه وسلم عَنِ البِرِّ وَ الأَثْمِ فَقَالَ البِرُّ حُسْنُ الخُلُقِ وَالاثْمُ مَا حَاكَ فِي صَدْرِكَ وَ كَرِهْتَ انْ يَطَّلِعَ عَلَيْهِ النَّاسُ.

AL-GHANEE

The Self-Sufficient

THE MESSENGER OF ALLAH, ^{peace and blessings of Allah be on him,} has said: "People will not sit in dhikr' Allah without the Angels surrounding them, mercy covering them, tranquility descending on them, and Allah mentioning them among those who are with Him."

[Reported by Abu Hurairah and Abu Sa'id]
[Transmitted by Muslim]

عَنْ اَبِي هُرَيْرَةَ وَ اَبِي سَعِيدٍ قَالَ قَالَ رَسُولُ اللهِ ﷺ لَا يَقْعُدُ قَوْمٌ يَذْكُرُونَ اللهَ اِلاَّ حَفَّتْهُمُ الْمَلَئِكَةُ وَ غَشِيَتْهُمُ الرَّحْمَةُ وَ نَزَلَتْ عَلَيْهِمُ السَّكِينَةُ وَ ذَكَرَهُمُ اللهُ فِيمَنْ عِنْدَهُ

AL-MUGHANI

The Enricher

THE MESSENGER OF ALLAH, ^{peace and blessings of Allah be on him,} has said: "He who repeats, *there is no god but Allah,* and he who does not are like the living and the dead."

[Reported by Abu Musa]
[Transmitted by Bukhari and Muslim]

Note: Remembering Allah (dhikr) indicates that one has forgotten him. Dhikr Daim (continuous dhikr) is remembering Allah in every action in life.

عَنْ أَبِى مُوسَى قَالَ قَالَ رسوُلُ اللهِ صلى الله عليه وسلم مَثَلُ الَّذِى يَذْكُرُ رَبَّهُ وَ الَّذِى لَا يَذْكُرُ مَثَلُ الحَيِّ وَ المَيِّتِ .

AL-MANI'

The Preventer

THE MESSENGER OF ALLAH, _{peace and blessings of Allah be on him,} has said: "When you pass the gardens of Paradise enjoy their fruits." They asked, "And what are the gardens of Paradise?" He said, "The circles of Dhikr."

عَنْ اَنَسٍ قَالَ قَالَ رسول الله صلى الله عليه وسلم اِذَا مَرَرْتُمْ بِرِيَاضِ الجَنَّةِ فَارْتَعُوا قَالُوا وَ مَا رِيَاضُ الجَنَّةِ قَالَ حَلَقُ الذِّكْرِ.

[Reported by Anas]
[Transmitted by Tirmizi]

Note: There are three degrees of Paradise. The first is obtained by repeating the names of Allah; the second is obtained by good actions in life and the third, which is the highest, is obtained by good actions from every aspect of oneself.

1. The dhikr of tongue.
2. The dhikr of action.
3. The dhikr of one's whole being.

AD-DAAR

The Distresser

THE MESSENGER OF ALLAH, ^{peace and blessings of Allah be on him,} has said: "There is a polish for everything and the polish of the heart is the remembrance of Allah."

[Reported by 'Abdullah ibn 'Umar]

[Transmitted by Ahmad]

Note: In the Qur'an Allah says, "Mention Me so that I mention you." If you mention His mercy, He will show you mercy, if you seek His love, He will show you His love.

عَنْ عَبْدِ اللهِ بْنِ عُمَرَ عَنِ النَّبِيِّ صلى الله عليه وسلم اَنَّهُ كَانَ يَقُولُ لِكُلِّ شَيْءٍ صِقَالَةٌ وَ صِقَالَةُ الْقُلُوبِ ذِكْرُ اللهِ . . . .

AN-NAAFI'

The Propitious

THE MESSENGER OF ALLAH, _{peace and blessings of Allah be on him,} has said: "He is one and loves unity."

[Reported by Abu Hurairah]
[Transmitted by Bukhari and Muslim]

Note: Unity is thinking of Him as one, and all mankind as part of that one.

عَنْ أَبِي هُرَيْرَةَ فِي رِوَايَةٍ وَهُوَ وِتْرٌ يُحِبُّ الوِتْرَ.

AN-NOOR

The Light

THE MESSENGER OF ALLAH, ^{peace and blessings} ^{of Allah be on him,} has said: ''There are ninety-nine names for Allah. Whoever repeats them will enter Paradise.''

[Reported by Abu Hurairah]
[Transmitted by Bukhari and Muslim]

عَنْ اَبِى هُرَيْرَةَ قَالَ قَالَ رَسُولُ اللهِ صلى الله عليه وسلم أَنَّ لِلّهِ تَعَالَى تِسْعَةً وَتِسْعِينَ أَسْمَاً مِائَةً اِلاَّ وَاحِدًا مَنْ أَحْصَاهَا دَخَلَ الْجَنَّةَ .

Note: If this repetition is only done with the tongue one may get tired.Just as a person may repeat the word bread, this alone does not mean he will eat. Nevertheless he should repeat bread, so that he may be heard and given what he asks. Unless one mentions the names of Allah with his tongue and his heart he will not be given Nur (Light) the bread of Allah,which enters the heart and is then dispersed to the rest of the body.

Allah is closer to man than he is to himself, but we are not close to Him. For this reason he has given us His names to repeat so that we may come closer to Him.

AL-HAADI

The Guide

THE MESSENGER OF ALLAH, _{peace and blessings of Allah be on him,} has said: ''To say,'There is no might and no power except in Allah,' is a medicine for ninety-nine diseases, the least of them being anxiety.''

[Reported by Abu Hurairah]
[Transmitted by Ahmad]

عَنْ اَبِى هُرَيْرَةَ قَالَ قَالَ رسولُ اللهِ لَاحَوْلَ وَ لَا قُوَّةَ اِلاَّ بِاللهِ دَوَاءٌ مِنْ تِسْعَةٍ وَ تِسْعِينَ دَاءٍ اَيْسَرُهَا الْهَمُّ

AL-BADEE'I

The Incomparable

THE MESSENGER OF ALLAH, peace and blessings of Allah be on him, has said: "When you see a man endowed with asceticism and speaks little, go to him for he has been given wisdom."

[Reported by Abu Hurairah and Abu Khallad]
[Transmitted by Baihaqi]

عَنْ اَبِي هُرَيْرَةَ وَ اَبِي خَلَّادٍ اَنَّ رَسُولَ اللهِ ﷺ قَالَ اِذَا رَأَيْتُمُ الْعَبْدَ يُعْطَى زُهْدًا فِي الدُّنْيَا وَ قِلَّةَ مَنْطِقٍ فَاقْتَرِبُوا مِنْهُ فَاِنَّهُ يُلَقَّى الْحِكْمَةَ.

AL-BAAQI

The Everlasting

THE MESSENGER OF ALLAH, ^{peace and blessings of Allah be on him,} has said: ''Shall I not inform you about who is best among you? The best of you are those who, when seen, reminds one of Allah.''

[Reported by Asma' bint Yazid]
[Transmitted by Ibn Majah]

عَنْ اَسْمَاءَ بِنْتِ يَزِيدَ سَمِعْتُ
رَسُولَ اللهِ عَلَيْهِ وَسَلَّمَ يَقُولُ اَلاَ اُنَبِّئُكُمْ
بِخِيَارِكُمْ قَالُوا بَلَى يَا رَسُولَ اللهِ قَالَ
اَخْيَارُكُمُ الَّذِينَ اِذَا رُؤُوا ذُكِرَ اللهُ .

AL-WAARITH

The Supreme Inheritor

THE MESSENGER OF ALLAH, ^{peace and blessings of Allah be on him,} has said: "Two or more form a congregation."

[Reported by Abu Musa al-Ash'ari]
[Transmitted by Ibn Majah]

عَنْ اَبِي مُوسَى الْاَشْعَرِيّ قَالَ قَالَ رَسُولُ اللهِ صلى الله عليه وسلم اِثْنَانِ فَمَا فَوْقَهَا جَمَاعَةٌ.

AR-RASHEED

The Guide to the Right Path

'Umar ibn al-Khattab reported: "Truly invocation is kept in abeyance between heaven and earth and nothing ascends until you send blessings on your Prophet."

[Transmitted by Tirmizi]

عَنْ عُمَرَبْنِ لِلْخَطَّابِ قَالَ اِنَّ الدُّعَاءَ مَوْقُوفٌ بَيْنَ السَّمَاءِ وَ الْأَرْضِ لَا يَصْعُدُ مِنْهُ شَىْءٌ حَتَّى تُصَلِّىَ عَلَى نَبِيِّكَ.

AS-SABOOR

The Patient

Abdullah ibn 'Amr reported that whoever sends one blessing to the Prophet, Allah and His angels send seventy blessings to him.

[Transmitted by Ahmad]

عَنْ عَبْدِ اللهِ بْنِ عَمْرٍ وَقَالَ مَنْ صَلَّى عَلَى النَّبِيِّ صَلَّى اللهُ عَلَيْهِ وَسَلَّمَ وَاحِدَةً صَلَّى اللهُ عَلَيْهِ وَمَلَئِكَتُهُ سَبْعِينَ صَلوةً.

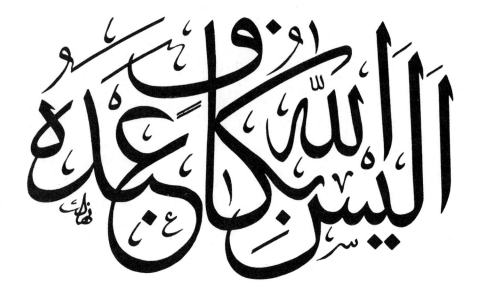

Isn't Allah sufficient for His servant !